# ART HIRING

## Beats selling!

**Graeme Smith**

PUBLISHED ON AMAZON.com
by
LABYRINTH BOOKS

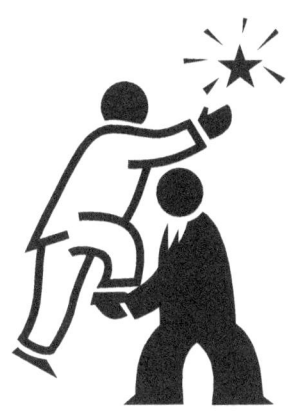

## DEDICATION:

This book is dedicated to my family.
> **Hele-ly (Ly).**
>> my wife:

> **Ingrid.**
>> our daughter:

> **Marie.**
>> my former wife:

> **Fiona, Natalie and Michael**
>> our children:

> **Georgie**
>> Michael's wife:

> **Pearl, Kiki and Martha.**
>> their children:

They have had to put up with me for many years and I thank them for that.
I hope this book gives an insight into what occupied me much of the time.
They have all achieved worthwhile and interesting careers.
In the absence of much help from me.
I congratulate them for their achievements.

**THANKS:**

**I greatly appreciate the contribution made to this book by comments and suggestions from:**

Mike Barr – Adelaide, Australia

Richard Bruland - Los Angeles, USA

Tracey Creighton - Merimbula, Australia

Evelyn Dunphy – Maine, USA

Geoff Fellows – Wagga Wagga, Australia

Michelle Grace - Brisbane, Australia

Leanne Halls – North Sydney, Australia

Heidi Jeffries – Ferny Hills, Australia

Kathy Kay Voysey - Mudgee, Australia.

Vince Miller – 'Australian Artist' and 'International Artist'.

John Newell - Ontario, Canada

David Voigt – Yarramalong, Australia.

# HOW TO USE THIS BOOK.

**First think - then do.**
Usually people don't think through things to the level they need to.
Because of that, they have projects instead of tasks on their "to do" list.
That leads to procrastination as it hasn't been broken down to a task level.

**So go through your book once to understand it.**
Go through it again.

**Then start at the idea you would like to implement first.**
Make notes of the steps you will need to take and the resources required.
Use these notes to create a step by step system for implementing the guide.
Often you will not refer back to an original, as you've created YOUR system.

**The first question you ask and answer is "Why is this being done?"**
How does this align with where you want to get to?
What are the strategic implications of doing this?
Does this fit with getting to a goal in the shortest and fastest amount of time?

**What would it be like if it were totally successful?**
Define it - what is success for this project and how will you know?

**Now brainstorm all the tasks that are involved in your project.**
It's important not to go linear too fast with this.
By linear, I mean step one, step two, step three, and step four.
You end up cutting off options.
Plan step one, two, and three, a specific step that might be number four.
If you start steps quickly, other ways of one, two or three may not appear.

**The first third of any brainstorming session is really easy.**
Just come up with lots of ideas.
The second third is challenging - go through ideas and see where they lead.
Then push yourself to think a little bit outside the box.
That's often where the big idea is!

**That's where the most powerful way to get a project done fastest - is.**
Most people never get to that level and end up short-changing themselves.
Then their project takes longer and they also procrastinate.
This final brainstorming part of the equation is incredibly important.

**Once you fully brainstorm put your options into a linear sequence.**
Then you can figure out what you've overlooked.
Everything becomes obvious as you get your tasks in order.
Now add missing steps and you have laid out your task list for this project.

**Once you've organized the tasks into a linear process decide:**
What things can you start immediately?
What can be started that is not dependent on things to occur before them?
Obviously that is step one.
Step five or six or twenty that don't really rely on anything else to get done.
You can get started on them right away too.

**Now use a folder.**
Write things you think of at the time and also cross off things as you do them.
Add in stuff that is relevant from time to time.

# WHAT IS MARKETING?

**Marketing is the process of finding buyers AND making sales**
It is exactly the same process no matter what is being sold!
In some cases the process is simple like selling apples at a roadside stall.
It can be very complex like selling aero-planes for a government's air-force.
Most, including selling artworks, is somewhere in between these poles.

**Think about fishing and you'll understand marketing.**
Does a fisherman catch anything out in a desert?
NO, for there are simply no fish there.

**You must market where there are possible buyers.**
A fisherman must go where the fish are – where there is water.
That's a start but there are still no fish in a swimming pool are there?
They need to be in the right kind of water – a river, lake or at sea.

**But different fish swim in different waters!**
Sharks and marlin are in the ocean, while bream live mainly in rivers.
Likewise you must know who you are targeting with your marketing.
Will it be businesses, first home buyers, investors or what?
Each will need a different marketing program.

**OK you are now in the right water for the kind of fish you are after!**
Some species are nocturnal and they will not be caught during the day.
Your marketing needs to be when the target is likely to be most receptive.
Will it be at work, nights or weekends?

**You are at the right place and time so how do you catch the fish?**
Usually you'll have a fishing rod.
Is it the right kind for the fish you want to catch?
You won't catch a shark with the kind of rod that takes a trout!
Your marketing must be attractive to the people you are after.

**Do you have the right bait?**
Again different bait attracts different fish.
A carcass for the shark but just a worm for many other species.
Can you provide something that your target market will find attractive?

**But throwing any bait into the water catches nothing at all!**
The bait must be attached to a hook.
Without the fish taking the hook there is no catch.
Different hooks are needed for different kinds of fish.

**Different hooks are also needed for different markets.**
The right hook gets your market to take the next step to a purchase.
But this only needs to be a little step.

**But hooks only catch the fish.**
They're in the water, not your boat or beach, a hook is on the end of a line.
What is your line like, is it strong enough you the fish you are after?
Again this varies for the kind of fish.

**How do you get your prospect to seriously consider what you sell?**
For someone buying a print it will not need to be sophisticated.
But selling an original Renoir will be considerably more complicated.

**That still no fish for the line has to have a reel for that to happen.**
Again different reels for different fish.
The right reel allows you to bring the fish to the end of your fishing line.
But it's still not in the boat is it?

**You must lift the fish out of the water into your boat or onto the beach.**
Fishing nets do this so now you have your catch.
The fish is yours to do what you want with.

**You can even sell the fish but who might want to buy?**
It could be someone who sells fish for food or live for a fish-tank or pool.
They could even be for re-stocking natural water places.

**Where can you find them?**

You must look where the fish buyers are so follow the path of the fisherman.

And eventually you have a prospect asking can they buy.

You have made a sale AND you can make more sales the same way.

**Making the sale is a five step process.**

In order you work from the top through to the bottom group.

> **SUSPECTS** are people who possibly want what you have for sale.
>
> **PROSPECTS** are people likely to want what you have for sale.
>
> **BUYERS** are those who have bought what you are selling.
>
> **REPEAT BUYERS** continue to buy what you sell.
>
> **ADVOCATES** help you sell to others.

**The reverse sequence is the order of importance to your sales.**

## INDEX: HIRING BEATS SELLING.

Chapter One: Your career vision.                          15
Chapter Two: Depending on an income from art?             20
Chapter Three: Art for business?                          26
Chapter Four: A look at hiring.                            36
Chapter Five: Selling the hiring.                          58
Chapter Six: Tools.                                        76
Chapter Seven: Wrapping up.                                94


**WHERE NEXT?**          **98**
**NOT NOW:**             **99**
**SEND TO:**             **100**

# Chapter One: Your career vision.

1. Do you have a long term vision about your career?
2. Something I learned from my gallery.
3. What's stopping you?
4. I assume you are interested in making money as an artist.

## 1. Do you have a long term vision about your career?

**Most artists tend to focus on an individual painting.**
An exhibition is a collection of their paintings.
But what if the focus is on the exhibition, as one of a series of exhibitions?
Then there's a different mind-set.

**There are other ways to leverage major career momentum too.**
But you still need sales and marketing strategies.

**You can't turn an art business into a successful** career overnight.
You just can't skip the fundamental steps needed **for a solid business.**

**You've got to be patient too!**
Even if you do things right, you can't do them all concurrently.
That means there is no short cut to success.
A professional artist is not merely a painter - that is what makes an artist.
You are also in business, or have a career, or in a profession.

**Money is a measure of how well you do.**
It's not the motivation, that's your desire to follow your dream.
But it does say something about how well you've followed the dream.
It also makes achieving your dream more feasible.

**It's unlikely better income leads to better work.**
But it leads to a better lifestyle.
You can live in a garret in poverty or have whatever lifestyle you'd like.
Either way your work will remain of much the same standard.

**Often artists assume the artwork sells itself.**
People fall in love with the work.
Marketing is a matter of putting people in front of paintings (exhibition).
Instead of blaming your painting for a failure to sell question the marketing.
Was there a failure to influence people's opinion in relation to your paintings?
Possibly there was a failure to find out what opinions were held to start with?

**But you have to earn money so YOU need to master marketing!**
Most artists think very little about marketing.
They hand it over to someone else hoping they know what to do.
But many of those people do **NOT** know what to do.

**Most people do not have a clue about most things they buy!**
When you shop for anything how specific is your 'decision-making' criteria?
How expert are you in areas like law, bedding, accountancy, or real estate?
Probably not much at all and therein is an extraordinary opportunity.

**Most potential buyers do not have highly sophisticated buying criteria.**
They have an idea what the prospective purchase could do for them.
They might even know what they paid in the past and that's about it!

**That means you can re-set the buying criteria for your entire market.**
Most people come to buying situations (your art) with flexible buying criteria.
Can you make your works their most logical choice?
And at the same time provide the best financial result for you.
All this without changing what you paint!

## 2. Something I learned from my gallery.

**I had a gallery years ago and after a few years I exhibited my own work.**
In one of those early exhibitions I had 50 works and sold the lot!

**I was approached by a restaurant owner to borrow some paintings.**
He said he could sell them to his customers.
I didn't like that idea for his customers were there to eat not buy artworks.
Also the lighting was to provide ambience for the restaurant.
It wasn't to display artworks!

**I countered with a proposal that he hire some artworks from my gallery.**
We did that and it worked out OK until the restaurant closed its doors.

**That started me thinking about how to do art hiring (renting) properly.**
It took a few years before I worked out exactly what to do.

**Nothing is going to happen until you do something.**
Just thinking and dreaming gets nothing done!
The toughest part is deciding what to do **FIRST – THEN** you **MUST** act.
Many people just waste time for they try to work out the best thing to do.
It is better to start and then turn that into the best thing you can.
Then procrastination becomes a thing of the past as well!

**It is actually better to do something even without goals.**
Than to just spend time deciding on goals and not actually doing anything.
You can fix wrong choices but if nothing is done then no change is made.
It's the status quo.

**When you make big major changes it's easy to get overwhelmed.**
It's easy to become discouraged and give up.
You revert to your old easy ways and say 'It's too hard!'
You blame yourself for your failure but it doesn't have to be like that.
Just take things one step at a time and other habits start to develop.

**Even the busiest person can find the time to take a single step.**

That's all it takes to get started!

Then you don't feel overwhelmed.

You make gradual but lasting changes to your career.

So choose a goal that you'd like to have happen in 30 days.

By taking it one step at a time generate momentum to achieving that goal.

**It could be the most important single step you can take consistently.**

Provided it will move you towards that goal.

**BUT** even doing what seems easiest might be a good way to start!

**3. I assume you are interested in making money as an artist.**

**One way is hiring to business unsold works or works specially for hire.**
Money earned from hiring is additional to any money you currently earn!

**Sales income forgone is covered in the first two years of hiring usually.**
After that money received is pure profit which can continue for many years.
Each additional hiring contract multiplies your profit.
And you still own the works hired out.

**Your profit compounds when you rehire works hired previously.**
These are works that have been partly or fully paid for already.
There is **NO** cost attached to them.

**Later hiring can be at current (i.e. later) values as well.**
Additional referrals increase the number of hiring contracts you can sell.
Even better a hiring contract is usually for multiple works.

**Hiring or renting is a generator of passive income.**
Once the contract is signed the money comes in at regular intervals.
On holidays, sick, retired or otherwise occupied and money still comes.
Now you have a balance to the typical variable income cycle of an artist.
This income can continue even when you are no longer active as an artist.

# Chapter Two: Depend on income from art?

### 1. Art investors aim to earn big money.
### 2. The world of art collecting can be a difficult business.
### 3. What is necessary for improved income?

## 1. Art investors aim to earn big money.

**Amy Yuen hopes to make a financial return on her painting.**
'The first time I saw this picture, I liked it,' says Amy Yuen.
Amy is a Hong Kong entrepreneur.
The Crying Baby Series One by a controversial Chinese artist, Yin Jun.
'I liked the details, I liked the mixture of colours.'

**She also liked the price:**
HK$168,000 (£13,100, $21,540), and potential to make money renting it out.

**Ms Yuen is one of a fast-growing group of first-time investors in art.**
They take a typically hard-headed Hong Kong approach to art.
She buys shares, property, project financing - not a mainstream investment

**The painting is far too big for her flat in Hong Kong.**
But she never intended it as decoration as it's perfect for a hotel or a bank.

**Ms. Yuen says she'll get a return of six% a year renting to such clients.**
'People who appreciate art will be able to appreciate it,' she says.
Hong Kong banks typically pay less than half a per cent interest on deposits.

**She's not sentimental: she thinks she'll sell the painting after 3 years.**
In that time, she forecasts its value will increase by 15 to 20% a year.
'I consider this as an alternative investment,' she says.

**'It will help to balance my portfolio.**
I'm planning to buy more art pieces in order to diversify.'

**The UK's nationalized rail company invested in art in the 1970s.**
Its pension fund invested $100m - around 2.5% of its portfolio - in artworks.
That included 25 Impressionist paintings, and more than 2,000 other items.
They ranged from African tribal art to Chinese ceramics.

**The pension fund started to sell its collection in 1987.**
They had disposed of it all by 1999.
It reportedly made a compound return of 11.3 per cent a year.

Auctioneers and brokers tell stories of people who buy paintings cheaply.
They sell later for millions when the artist has become famous.
But in real life, such luck is rare for there are many pitfalls to investing in art.
Even experts can be fooled by fakes.

**Shares can be sold in a matter of hours.**
Paintings can take a long time to sell; years even.
Auction houses and galleries may charge high fees for their services as well.
Art critics have their darlings, which history may cruelly forget.
An investment guru John Train says this in his book The Craft of Investing.

**The art establishment can be poor judges of what has lasting value.**
In the late 19th century no winners of the prestigious Prix de Rome in Paris
Judges felt no painter was worthy of the award in 1888 or 1897.
Degas, Cezanne, Matisse, Monet, Renoir, Toulouse-Lautrec all exhibited.

**That said, art does have some attractive features as an investment.**
Research suggests generally prices of paintings keeps pace with inflation.
That protects savings from losing their value in real terms.
Buying art to rent to businesses also generates cash.

## 2. The world of art collecting can be a difficult business.

### Buying art can be a frustrating experience if you're new to it.
There are lots of shops and websites selling mass-produced prints.

### Buying original work can involve more leg work.
It requires trips to multiple galleries and trawling art websites.
But the biggest challenge for the prospective buyer is being taken seriously.
Particularly if you're not already been priced out of the market – a beginner.

### A website in USA gives collectors a chance to 'try before you buy'.
They can rent the art first.
Twenty-four-year-old New Yorker Alexis Tyron had just that problem.
Two years ago she went to a gallery armed with her chequebook.
She was ready to buy a work she had researched and could afford.
All she wanted to do was see it for herself.

### They wanted her back but an appointment was Tuesday afternoon.
But she has a job so couldn't come in on a Tuesday afternoon.
She tried to pay $1000 (£623) but wasn't taken seriously by the gallery.
Alexis is a young professional.
Her friends were having the same sort of challenges.

### So she started online offering accessible, affordable, original art.
For $50 (£31) a month, art lovers can choose a painting, sculpture or print.
There is a collection of 30 emerging and more established artists.

### They hang in their homes to decide if they like it enough to buy or not.
If they do, they can buy the work - prices are from $500 - $5,000.
If they don't, they can send it back or rent another one.

### Tyron also aims to address the fear of buying art online.
How do you know what it will look like in your home?
She lets collectors live with the work for a while.

**There is no sense of having to go somewhere to find the artwork.**
Instead there is a group who have become affiliated.
She lets people she worked with or knew keep her works for 3 weeks before.
Leasing is brilliant Tyron says if collectors have doubts if a work is right.
Leasing lets them address the doubts in a way that is respectful of the artist.

**Galleries create a strong, healthy and resilient market for the artist.**
In interest of an artist's career their works are with the best person possible.
That's to do with the artist's and gallery's reputation.
It's not possible in many cases to just walk into a gallery and buy something.
In a typical gallery there are no prices and you have to request a price sheet.
A range of paintings, sculptures and prints are available for prospects
Clients buy works because they like them, not as a potential goldmine.

**The basis for this article supplied by Rosemary Antell (Seattle USA)**

### 3. What is necessary for improved income?

**In spite of a widely held belief your artwork doesn't sell itself.**
If it did, you'd could hang your work up anywhere and people would buy it.
However you may have experienced good sales in the past.
Other artists have major sales in galleries in different parts of the world.
But these days it's a little different.

**You still need the security of regular income so what holds you back?**
You know you have to do something different but aren't sure what.

**Do you have a large stock of unsold works?**
Many artists have a collection of their own works.
Usually they are works that have failed to find a buyer.
At the time you thought them satisfactory and some were your favourites.
Gradually they become dated and are considered old works (at least by you).
Often they are unframed for that has gone to another work.

**Could these unsold works form the basis for improved income?**
It would depend what you do with them wouldn't it?
Would you make a major effort to earn money from those unsold works?
You would if your net income is **NOT** high enough.

**BUT you need a money making solution to the problem of not selling!**
Your sales need not involve any change in ownership!
Your sales could be to provide the pleasure of contemplation of the works.
In other words you can sell **USE** rather than **OWNERSHIP**.
You have a product (your artwork), and a client wants to own it.
You don't want to sell to them as you want to retain ownership yourself.
Your client pays a fee to use your work, rather than own it like leasing a car.

**Actually it's more like hiring a car.**
It's also like using the operating system that comes with your PC or MAC.
You don't own that operating system; it's licensed from Microsoft or Apple.
That's why you can't resell your operating system to someone else.

# Chapter Three: Art for business?
### 1. What about art for business?
### 2. What do businesses buy?
### 3. Hiring is an alternative income source.


## 1. What about art for business?

**Often businesses are perceived to be potential buyers of artwork.**
There is artwork on walls of businesses in TV news stories and drama shows.
In fact often there are quite a number of artworks shown in these situations.
How do you get your works onto those walls, or ones like them?
It's a tantalizing prospect isn't it?

**The main information for artists is about selling their work.**
It's through galleries, art shows and privately, to individual buyers.
Occasionally buyers are businesses, with a gallery likely to have the contact.
There's little on selling to business we assume it's the same as private sales.
It's not easy.
In some ways that assumption is correct, but in some ways it is not.

**Business, of whatever sort, is about making money.**
The owner can do things that they otherwise (without money) could not do.
A business, because they're in business, is attracted by an investment angle
Implied is artwork is a worthy investment for them, the business concerned.

**So how can they make money on your artwork?**
Provide them with an answer and you are on the way to a sale to a business.
A gallery, interior decorator or picture framer have their own answer.
But you know about them, so I'll focus on other, non-art related businesses.

**Many businesses have potential art buyers as their clients.**
Some could be interested in an agent role, with a commission on sales made.
Motels, hotels, clubs, restaurants and similar are targets for this approach.
Those in a tourist area are worth approaching from that point of view.

**If dealing with this type of outlet, do it on a proper business basis.**
Your results could be disappointing if you don't.
There is a tendency for these places to see your work as free wall decoration.

**In Ottawa there are more artists per capita than anywhere in Canada.**
Art sales are the lowest in the country possibly for the same reason.
Many professional offices are provided with artwork free by their artist clients.
They want to exhibit their work and make a sale to a client of the business.

**Many restaurants in Ottawa have cottoned on to something.**
They get artwork for their walls without paying by offering space to artists.
Some restaurants take a commission on sales, some don't.
Exhibitions change monthly and plenty of artists fill the walls on regularly.

**But one gallery (at least) has a large corporate art rental business.**
So somewhere there, businesses **ARE** paying money and renting artwork.
They are not just obtaining it from artists free.

**Then there are TV and movie production companies?**
Artists can produce art for specific programs that suit the needs of the set.
An artist I know had a painting rented for the set of a TV mini-series.
She watched the program hoping to see her painting.
Unfortunately she became so engrossed in the plot that she missed her work.
She was paid for it being there, as did the gallery who rented it.

**The potential outlets above are just some of the most obvious ones.**
Any business that has wall space and a steady flow of people is a prospect.
They will be even better prospects if their clients, are likely to buy artwork.
Arrangements with a local social security office is unlikely to lead to sales.

**But works in a lawyer's office, or local tourist centre, could be better.**
Government offices are a complete waste of time.
Politicians and bureaucrats know how to get everything for free!
Corporate offices are a much better bet.

**Most businesses might buy art but the bottom line is paramount.**
A company won't usually spend money that doesn't help the finances.
So you need to demonstrate how this can be done to make a sale.
Art in the public office area is likely to be a non-starter.
If a focus is selling products on the internet or by salesmen who visit clients.
Clients visiting the office is a more likely prospect.

**Furniture stores may take art on consignment.**
They offer inexpensive, overpriced, mass-produced reproductions on canvas.
For uneducated buyers it's a no-brainer, pretty, cheap, can't tell difference.
Retail stores don't usually have space for anything that doesn't make money.

**Like people everywhere, most business is focused on its own interests.**
The smaller the business, the more obvious this is.
Even then it's possible to approach the small business on a personal basis.
It's likely the business is basically the person who owns it.
What works for individuals to see art worth buying, works for small business.
Similarly whatever fails, will fail here as well!

**Who buys?**
For a small business don't think they are a business, think of them as people.
What sort of benefit might they obtain from your artwork?
How can a work help them get love, pleasure, status or what they desire?

**Major companies are actually no different, if you get to the right people.**
That's a pretty big **IF** though.
The right people are the decision-makers.
This is obviously the 'boss', but sometimes there may be other right people.
It could be a purchasing officer, the boss's secretary, wife, or office manager.
Maybe some other individual could buy your artwork for the company?

**In this situation the first task is to track down the right person.**
You probably need to enlist others to help and also prepare the way for a sale.
This is time consuming, where many preliminary sales need to be made.

**Only then will the actual sale become possible.**
You need stamina and considerable personal relationship skill to achieve this.
Then approach that person on much the same basis as a smaller business.

**If you meet a decision-maker in a social context, the process is easier.**
Thus joining Rotary Clubs and the like could be a good business investment.
Get involved with high profile fundraisers who are the 'movers and shakers'.
These people like their photos in a society column of the local newspapers!

**The scale of a larger business may mean there's more money available.**
Particularly because it's not their own money that is being spent!
They buy something they wouldn't have at home for a business not their own.
On the other hand there may be a bank-like approach to the business.
There the $ value of everything done is carefully assessed.

**So what does that mean?**
You have to show the business, whatever its size, what's in it for them.
What do they gain buying and hanging one or more of your works on a wall?
If you say it'll be a worthy investment you demonstrate this to the business.

**But it can happen if an artist was paid to paint a mural of the local area.**
This was on the wall of an independently owned grocery store.
A pictorial map of the area and clients related to it and enjoyed their homes.

**Before this, a proposal is weighed against other worthy investments.**
This is what individual buyers do too.
At times when money is plentiful, people can attain most of their choices.

**As economic circumstances become difficult options attainable reduce.**
In the end, persuasion can't sell artwork to a business that has no money.

**They are interested in survival.**
Then you'll need to show these people how your art can help them survive!
A tough call, but it **can** be done.

**But hiring can save you time?**

You only have to paint a work once.

You can hire it repeatedly – if necessary to different people.

You can earn money from it for a long time without painting a new work.

Passive income from a broad hiring program means spend time how you like.

The money just keeps on coming and your time is free.

## 2. What do businesses buy?

**Corporations buy all manner of artworks.**
Some is for boardrooms and large and prestigious (i.e. pay a lot of money).

**Business also buys a great deal of other smaller less expensive works.**
These are for corridors, normal offices, etc.
However, these days most businesses have little money to waste.
They are thus less inclined to buy artworks than a few years ago.

**Are there problems for a business that buys artworks?**
It may be tax-deductible but the claim is not so easy to substantiate.
Depreciation also reduces attractiveness of this way of tax minimization.
Depending where you live, there might be capital gains tax down the track.
This is balanced by the ownership factor.

**Have you thought about hiring art to businesses?**
Our government here in Australia has.
Artbank is an institution that lends work to other government departments.
They also lend art to the non-government sector.
I imagine other countries have similar authorities and arrangements.
To lend artworks on the scale of Artbank requires a huge stock.
A lot of money is invested in inventory but you don't have to be on that scale.

**Any business likely to buy paintings is also a candidate for hiring.**
Waiting rooms, boardrooms, and offices where people look at blank walls.
Any business that's conscious of its image is a potential hiring client too.

**So why hire when you can sell?**
With renting or hiring, people pay, usually per month, for use of the paintings.
I had a number of works hired for over 17 years by a firm of solicitors.
Depending the hiring fee actual costs were covered in two and a bit years.
Everything from then on is pure profit, and I still owned the works!

**Say someone, who is in business, is contemplating buying a painting.**
Suggest they could buy or hire for business people are used to hiring.
They hire or rent cars, pot plants, furniture, office equipment, etc.
The business is paying for the use of these items, but not for ownership.
As a legitimate tax deduction hiring can be attractive for a business person.
A total, legal, tax-deductible expense, if the work is hung at the business.

**They're not stuck with works as they would be if were bought outright.**
Offer to take them back (exchange for others) after a period (six months).
It's a strong argument, and there is no worry if the selection is criticized.
This is often a concern for people unfamiliar with art.

## 3. Hiring is an alternative income source.

**Hire unsold works or produce works especially for hiring to business.**
Money earned from hiring activity is additional to money you currently earn!
Each additional hiring contract multiplies profit and you own the works hired.

**Instead of an exhibition paint works to be hired.**
Add unsold works from exhibitions to hire stock and so are no longer for sale.
I abstracted some works, and painted over others from an exhibition.

**Sales income forgone is covered in the first two or three years of hiring.**
Then money received is pure profit and that can continue for many years.

**Profit compounds as you rehire works hired previously at NO cost.**
Later hiring can be at current (later) values too.
Additional referrals increase the number of hiring contracts you can sell.
In addition usually a hiring contract is for multiple works.

**Hiring or renting is a generator of passive income.**
Once the contract is signed the money comes in at regular intervals.
You could be on holidays, sick, dead, or no longer an active artist.
But the money still comes in.

**Now you can balance to the typical variable income cycle of an artist.**
It's actually a way **YOU** can make more money.
The upward income spiral can continue for the duration of your career.
You are now the professional artist running your business.
There is very little to be gained by **MERELY READING** what I write.
To get **ANY** benefit you must actually **DO** something!

**Supplement your regular sales income with passive income.**
You **CAN** break the sales income cycle by opening up the business market!
Solve some of business problems.

**Create clients.**

To start with segment your contact list then you can get your mailings right!

**But you need an action plan for selling the hiring.**

Which clients will make your hiring business?

Do you keep photographic records?

Documentation is important so contracts are essential.

# Chapter Four: A look at hiring.

1. Have you experienced this rental proposal?
2. Can lending or hiring be better than selling for you?
3. It makes a great deal of sense to hire.
4. A business likely to buy paintings is a candidate for hiring.
5. Hiring provides passive income.
6. Why you should hire/rent.
7. Expanding your hire stock.
8. Additional notes.

## 1. Have you experienced this rental proposal?

**Recently I've heard about a rental proposal I'd treat very cautiously.**
There's nothing wrong with renting if you are happy with arrangements.
I'd actually prefer to rent paintings than sell them.

**An American artist reported an agent from Atlanta found her web site.**
Together with other artists, the agent is seeking paintings of San Francisco.
The proposal is not a big money maker, but every penny does help she says.
Ritz Carlton Hotel will rent the paintings and giclee prints of each as well.
In order to protect herself our artist has hers on a CD.

**Each artist involved is paid $25 per print, 8 prints per image or $200.**
The artist is sure the total cost for the hotel will be big.
After agents, decorators, framer and a little to the artists are all considered.
As she says, artists are usually happy for anything which comes their way.

**But paintings recorded on a digital disk can be copied.**
If they are copied for 8 they can be copied for a number the publisher wants.
This can be done without telling you.

**They are San Francisco images, the logical marketplace.**
An artist living in San Francisco might discover pirated prints (a big city).
But not if they were in Sydney which is a reassurance.

**In this particular case I believe the artist is being ripped off.**
When I rent out paintings the hotel, or wherever, is charged a monthly fee.
The same should be the case in any rental proposal, for that's what renting is.
In my case, an artwork worth (say) $1000 might be $20 per month.
This is for renting an original work and a similar process applies for prints.
Let's say five prints are worth $200 each the fee would be $20 per month.

**In the questionable proposal, the artist was offered $200.**
Translate this into what she gets and what the agent would get?
No doubt an agent should get something for setting up the arrangement.

**Probably the artist has been offered the first month's fee!**
In 12 months she will have made $200 (full stop).
The agent probably $2200.00 and increasing at the rate of $200 a month!

**I'd want 50/50 of the hotel's monthly payment for as long as they rent.**
The artist still owns the works.
She is receiving $200 to take her works off the market for an indefinite period.
I imagine the Ritz Carlton could afford to buy original artworks if they wanted.

**There is also likely to be a problem in relation to copyright.**
If the agent turns her works into prints then she must agree to that in writing.
She should earn something for it (maybe $25 each).
But with giclee, it's possible to run out more - later.
How will she know about that if it happens?

**It's a chance this can happen and if so she is entitled to more money.**
But you can only get this if you are aware of the extra prints.
As the previous paragraph illustrates this agent is a pretty smart operator.
There are more prints are on the cards I'd think.

**I think she won't be able to obtain any additional money from the agent.**
Because other artists are willing to supply their works for the peanuts on offer.

**But there could be some negotiation following some questions.**
How long will the hotel be renting?
What is their monthly fee?
Could put her in a stronger position to receive a better return.
Or threaten to inform other artists about the renting scam.

**Artists get ripped off because they don't do their sums and homework.**
Do you do your sums in regard to any proposal that arrives unexpectedly?
What would you do in this artist's situation?

## 2. Can lending or hiring be better than selling for you?

**Selling is great, but lending can be even better.**
Have you thought about hiring (or renting) art to other businesses?
In Australia Artbank is the government institution that lends work.
They lend to embassies, offices and government departments.
They also lend art to the non-government sector.
I imagine other countries have similar authorities and arrangements.

**Hiring is often attractive for a business person.**
A total and legal tax-deductible expense, if the work is hung in the business.
It's a similar arrangement to hiring cars, or pot plants, or furniture.
The business is paying for the use of these items, but not for ownership.

**But the main reason why they hire is they're not stuck with the works.**
Like they would be if they were bought outright.
So offer to take them back (exchange for others) after a period (six months).
They don't worry if a selection is criticized, a concern for some people.
If they change the works the price might remain the same.
But it can be altered by starting again with new pieces.
There will be a new contract (see elsewhere) for any changed arrangements.

**Offering to swap works is an important selling point.**
Many potential hirers feel they may get tired of the paintings after a while.
So they are relieved to know the paintings can be changed.
The longer they keep the works, the less likely they are to change them.
The works become a part of the character of the workplace and its identity.
In one case I had a number of works hired for over 17 years by a firm.

**Actually I prefer to hire, rather than sell my own works.**
Depending on your hiring fees, your actual costs are covered in a year or two.
Everything from then on is pure profit, and you still own the works!

**You can also offer to paint special works for the business to be hired.**
Thus you combine commissions with the corporate approach and hiring.

**Commissions are slightly higher than similar non-commissioned work.**
Are you likely to get back any work that was commissioned and then hired?
Your descendants will be collecting on this sort of arrangement.

**To lend artworks on the scale of Artbank requires a huge stock.**
A large amount  of money is invested in their inventory.
Fortunately you don't have to do things on quite that scale.
As a result of hiring artworks to businesses, I now have a stock of artworks.

**Eventually you'll wonder why you ever sold a single hired work.**
And then had to paint a replacement.
Manly it was because you didn't know any better.

### 3. It makes a great deal of sense to hire.

**Have works available to be hired by businesses.**
Someone in business, and is contemplating buying a painting, has a choice.
They can buy or hire.
But keep the "for sale" stock and the "hire" stock separate.
Otherwise a potential hirer/buyer calculates the real hiring cost.

**That means you need an inventory of works to hire out.**
Paint works specifically for this purpose, just as you would for an exhibition.
They are to be hired instead of sold may make a difference to what you paint.
That's an artistic matter but you need works to your hire inventory regularly.

**Don't forget any old unsold works you have (everybody has some).**
They are part of your hire stock at the same hire price as similarly sized work.
This is a much better than painting over (destroy if they're not your standard).
But then those works are no longer available for someone to buy.

**Add works by other artists to your inventory.**
Other artists works mean a greater range of hiring options than just yours.
The best way to obtain such work is to exchange your own for them.
No money changes hands but your hire stock has greater variety than before.

**In addition you will need some cheaper options for people.**
Prints bought from newsagents can be a cheap way to this stock source.
Another way is to buy old calendars usually cheap with excellent images.
Frame the images and you have a large stock for business people to choose.

**Standardize frames to three or four sizes so each print is matted to fit.**
In calculating hire cost of the prints frame cost is the major component.
Couple all these with your works and you're ready to start art hiring business.

**4. Any business likely to buy paintings is a candidate for hiring.**

**The best to approach have waiting rooms, boardrooms, and offices.**
Generally find areas where people sit and look at a blank wall.
Any business that's conscious of its image is a potential hiring client too.

**I wouldn't have signs showing the works are yours or can be bought.**
This is unprofessional.
The business is paying you to use these works, **NOT** as advertising for you.

**I don't allow my hire stock to be bought nor quote a selling price.**
I just say 'The work will cost $50 a month (or whatever) to hire.
Say the person selects a painting to hire from you.
If it's owned by another artist have an agreement to cover this situation.
Go ahead on the basis of a shared return from the hiring payments.

**For the other artist this is a little like a client paying off a work.**
Regular often small payments over lengthy periods, but still own the work.
Few artists are interested in this arrangement, but some are.
You'll have to negotiate with each artist to see what level of interest there is.

**A better approach is to pay the artist for a sale (price less commission).**
Install it in the office, board room or wherever, and they sign a contract,
Pay the artist once the client has agreed to hire the painting and you own it.
You receive all the money from this hiring arrangement.
If you are doubtful about this remember my solicitor client (17 years hiring).
Most of my hiring contracts last for three or four years, but many go longer.
Less than two years duration does happen but is not common.

**Don't forget follow up.**
Client follow up is important as it's easy to hire works and just collect money.
You still need to maintain your relationship with your client.
One way is to contact the client, say quarterly.
Make sure that they're still happy or they might need additional works.
This is an opportunity to update the business's plans for the future.

**There may be an opportunity to help them out if you** Keep track of them.
They're creating a new showroom, additional location, or closing a branch.
You can take charge of removing works and installing them in a new location.
If things are not going well so you might get your paintings out of there.

**Just so you get the idea let's take a hypothetical case.**
A work normally sells for $2000 (you get $1333 or less after commission).
Its hiring fee is, $40 a month (2% of value), so in a year you'll collect $480.
That amount covers frame, canvas, paint etc. (in other words your costs).

**Let's say your costs for this painting were $450.**
Then once this amount has been passed you are making a profit.
At the end of a second year you make $510 and after three years $990.
That is $107 more than your profit from a sale $1333 - $450.
There is another $480 profit for each additional year that the work is hired.

**If the hirer returns the work you can hire it out again.**
Depending how long it was hired there is probably no cost at all!
Profit from day one which is why you wouldn't sell but keep in your hire stock.
Otherwise you'd have to paint and frame a replacement.

**I'd rather add new paintings to my hire stock than replace ones sold.**
Whatever income you earn from hiring just keeps on coming.
This increases as more businesses hire rather than buy.
This income comes if you go on holiday, do not paint, or sick and can't paint.
It's called passive income – you don't have to spend time working to earn it.

**Build in incentives to encourage people to become long-term hirers.**
For example you can reduce the hiring fee each year.
You took $50 off annually for the first five years as a thank you for continuing.

**In the above example, it would cost $750 to do this (or maybe $250).**
In 5 years the client pays $1650 ($2400 less $750) continues at $130 a year.
They know you have given them a very good deal.
These amounts illustrate the kind of thing that can be done.

**Quoting monthly payments makes everything seem cheaper.**
It is thus psychologically more likely to gain a sale (well hire I mean).

**Another way is to lock in annual payments instead of monthly ones.**
For example you can quote an annual figure $480 rather than a monthly one.
A variation is a choice, this work can be hired for $50 a month or $480 a year.
Business people do sums so it won't be hard to know what option they take.

**You could also do quarterly or semi-annual payments too.**
They sound less than annual payments and may be more beneficial for you.
Larger payments several times a year, small monthly, or a big annual one.
Arrange annual payments from different clients to spread income out better.
This is what will eventually happen anyway.

**The longer the contract, the better the rate is.**
I aim to recover my share of cost of a work in two years (2/3 of retail price).
After that the work owes me $0 and any further hiring is 100% profit.
If you are hiring out your own works you could be even more generous.

**The business must accept liability for loss or damage.**
I developed a document based on a form used if leasing rental property.
It must be O.K.
I've hired to lawyers and real estate using the document with no questions.
They will not be able to get insurance cover for artworks they don't own.
But you can.
What do you do these days, when insurance charges are quite ridiculous?
Use your own judgment about that but I carry the risk and don't tell anyone.

## 5. Hiring provides passive income.

### What is passive income?
Rent or dividends are well known forms of passive income.
That's money coming in even when you are on holidays, sick or even dead!
Money arrives at regular intervals and you only need to set it up.
Your hire stock gives security of income and helps retirement and old age.
Understand and use hiring (renting) as a major strategy in your career.
Hiring artwork is **THE** major untapped strategy for artists.

### A hiring program starts slowly and you may wonder why you bother.
But after the first couple of years you will know why you do it.
It's the hedge against a falling sales graph.
For an artist in a slump hiring is the easiest way to turn a career around.

### Wait for the 'right' time and what happens is the process is delayed.
There needs to be much work actually done, before there is any return.
But there's little actual expense initially, particularly if you have unsold works.
So a start can be made provided time is available.
But if you put it off it will never happen so either do it or forget it!

### My hiring contracts last for three or four years but many were longer.
Less than two years is rare.
As a result of hiring artworks to businesses, I now have a stock of artworks.
Many are earning me money on a regular basis.

### What rental does the business pay?
The simple answer is whatever you convince them to pay.
My fees are mainly based on the size of the work.
But the size, nature of the work, and duration of the hiring contract are linked.
I don't tell the client the retail price.

### Here's how to calculate your hiring fee.
What size is the work?

**It will be one of four sizes (big, medium, standard and small).**
Allocate all hired works into one of those sizes.
Is the work under glass or not?

**That is it!**

**Every work is allocated a standard price according to that formula.**
Do not worry about what you paid or could sell the work for.
This is how you decide what someone pays to hire the work.
If hired out sufficiently all works are eventually paid for.

**The longer the contract the better (lower) the rate could be.**
Usually I recover my share of the cost in two years (2/3 of the retail price).
After that the work owes me $0 and any further hiring is 100% profit.
But sometimes with an expensive work it takes longer to recover the cost.
If you are hiring out your own works you could be even more generous.

**Generally people pay me about 2% per month.**
**Suggested CONTRACT duration and related charges:**
**LESS THAN 36 MONTHS:** 2% per month of current value at time of hiring.
**MORE THAN 36 MONTHS**: 1.5% per month of current value at time of hire.

**Just so you get the idea let's take a hypothetical case.**
A work sells for $2000.
You get $1333 or less after deducting gallery commission.
Its hiring fee is $40 a month (2% of the value), so in a year you receive $480.
That covers your frame, canvas, paint etc. (in other words your costs).

**Let's say your costs for this painting were $450.**
Once this amount has been passed you are making a profit.
At the end of a second year you've made $510.
At the end of the third year $990.
This is $107 more than your profit from a sale ($1333 - $450).
You continue making $480 for each additional year that the work is hired.

**This might seem a little confusing so I'll try to explain with more clarity.**
Original cost: 4 works @$450 each (not my paintings that's what I paid).
Hire = ($9 per painting per month) $36 per month payment.
But $3.15 per painting per month was tax deductible at a rate of 35%
Real hiring cost = ($9 - $3.15 = $5.85 a painting a month) or $23.40 a month.

**There's no extra cost for rise in value of paintings in the hiring period.**
Several years down the track the client could be hiring four $900 works.
**BUT** the actual outlay is $23.40 per month (calculated value $450 each).
Later you could reduce long-term clients' fees further as illustrated below.

**BUT it may only be necessary to point out the capital gains values.**
You demonstrate the increasing value to the client of continued hiring.
It will cost more to replace these works with equivalent valued works!
Interest is on money not spent, rate of appreciation of artworks, and inflation.

**You can build in incentives to encourage people to be long-term hirers.**
You take $50 off a year for the first five years as a thank you for continuing.
In the above example, it would cost $250 to do this.
However in five years your client has paid $2150 ($2400 less $250).
They continue at $430 a year forever, knowing you gave them a good deal.
You needn't use these amounts; they just illustrate what you could do.

**Another way is to lock in annual payments rather than monthly ones.**
For example you can quote an annual figure $480 rather than a monthly one.
You could also suggest quarterly or semi-annual payments too.
That sounds less than annual payments and perhaps more beneficial for you.
A payment several times a year instead of small monthly or big annual fee.

**A variation is to provide a choice.**
This work can be hired for $50 a month or $480 a year.
Business people do sums so you know the option they'll take.
**BUT** quoting monthly payments makes everything seem cheaper.
It is thus psychologically more likely to gain a sale (well hire I mean).

With **enough works hired out, you'll then have a regular income stream.**
This irons out the ebb and flow of normal art-world business transactions.
Old unsold works you have (everyone has some) can be in your hire stock.
**BUT** they attract the same hire price, as any other similarly sized new work.
It makes a great deal of sense to do this if it's at all possible.

**Arrange annual payments from different clients in different months.**
This spreads your income out although that will eventually happen anyway.

## 6. Why you should hire/rent.

**Move from thinking of yourself as an artist to a marketer of your art.**
Then it isn't just about selling what you paint!

**Marketing is about everything you do that can earn income as an artist.**
Marketing and selling **IS** your business.
If you don't know what business you're really in you'll **NEVER** be successful!
You **MUST** embrace the reality you are actually in marketing and sales.
Then things can change because your mind-set will be different.

**You'll probably resist this due to accumulated experience and habit.**
Like most other artists you are used to doing things in a certain way.
This way is just the same as all the other artists!
You think about yourself as an artist rather than as a business person.
You also think your job is to paint artworks and then sell them.
Maybe someone else does the selling.

**When you think like a business person new possibilities emerge.**
One possibility is you can make money without even selling the work.
The work can earn income that comes in regularly.

**The real cost of hiring is not as great as often thought.**
The client's outlay is reduced by the business tax rate (which varies).
Tax is at the full hiring amount paid as it's a legitimate business expense.
It is not a reduced `buy-out' figure (as in leasing).

**Offering to exchange works is an important selling point too.**
Many potential hirers feel they may get tired of the paintings after a while.
So they are relieved to know the paintings can be changed.

**The longer they keep the works, the less likely they are to change.**
The works become part of the character of the workplace and its identity.

**In addition hiring is one way to earn money from your frames.**
Usually frames are a cost, reimbursed if a work is sold but many never are!
The main risk with this strategy is initially you're out of pocket (what's new?).

**But you do not need to frame all works for hire/rental.**
Just a small selection of standard sized frames are needed.
**As they are hired they can be replaced.**

**Your frames for hiring should be in standard sizes.**
Thus only a limited number of frames are required (see elsewhere).
Usually your hire stock will be unframed.
Works on paper are matted so they fit easily into your standard sized frame.

**Frame hired works to match the decor of the business environment.**
These works are likely to stay hired for a very long time.
Because they will look as if they belong in that environment.
But use standard sizes so if necessary other works can use the frames later.

**Thus you will have a great deal of unframed work.**
These are likely to be cheaper lines (posters, prints, calendar pages, etc.).
Different mat-boards can marry the range of works on paper to your frames.

**Then hiring earns money from framing.**
Whatever fee you receive is mainly for the frame as prints etc. are cheap.
You also have some cheaper options for public areas, corridors and motels.

**What if the hirer returns the work?**
If they change the works the price might remain the same.
**BUT** it could alter by starting again with current prices for a similar work.
Special frames are in standard sizes so all works fit one or another of them.

**You hire a returned work and there's no cost linked to the work at all!**
Profit from day one!
That's also why you wouldn't sell but instead retain them in your hire stock.
This will save you painting and framing replacements.

**I'd rather add new paintings to my hire stock, than replace ones sold.**
Whatever income you earn from hiring just keeps on coming.
It's added to as more businesses hire rather than buy.
This income comes if you go on holiday, do not paint, or are sick and can't.
You'll wonder why you bothered to sell a work and then paint a replacement.

**You can also offer to paint special works to be hired by the business.**
Thus you combine commissions with the corporate approach and hiring.
Commissions have a slightly higher fee than similar non-commissioned work.
Are you likely to get back any work that was commissioned and then hired?
Your descendants will be collecting on this sort of arrangement.

**Once I was approached by an owner to paint his horse.**
I did this and they were happy.
Then the son of the owner of the most celebrated horse in this part of
Australia approached me.
The horse had won many more races in its career than any other.
His father was turning 70.
The son wanted to give him a painting of the famous horse.
I accepted this commission on the basis of my previous experience.

**I went to the stable and saw the horse and developed the painting.**
My commissioner loved it and payment was made.
Possibly you have had a similar experience.

**I got thinking about commissions and painting horses.**
At that point I could have developed a career as an equine artist.
There are certain kinds of paintings that are mainly commissioned.
Having exhibitions of this kind of work will usually fail.
Not due to inferior work but rather because the work is not specific enough.

**The more specific the work the more appealing to a particular buyer.**
They commission such works and also pay higher prices!
They will also hire the right work and keep it for a long time!

## 7. Expanding your hire stock.

**Hire out your own artwork and there are limits to expanding income.**
Some potential hirers may not like what you do.
**In addition it takes time to paint additional works.**
There may be better ways to spend that time.
Expand your hiring client base for example.

**But what if you buy other artists works?**
Then you can provide alternatives to your own work.
You also have many more works available to choose from than otherwise.

**But buying other artist's works can be expensive!**
Well it all depends what you buy and how you do it.

**Most artists have unsold works (even you but yours are for hiring out).**
Make an offer for the works which otherwise are not earning the artist money.
In fact they have cost time and money already.

**The major money component of an unsold work is the frame.**
An artist can use the frames for other works and save on buying new frames.
Recycling frames is actually quite common.
So many of the unsold works are unframed.

**Unframed works should be considerably cheaper than if framed.**
This should be OK with a seller as they can use the frames on new works.
They save money.
This suits you too.

**Buying unframed works is less expensive for you.**
But buying in bulk should be even more inexpensive.
You remove a psychological problem for the seller (unsold reminder).
They also have frames available for new works.

## But what do you pay?

You must be able to hire the works and make money on the arrangement.

Your hiring fees are set according to the size of the works.

So your purchase offer is based on the same principle.

## What do you offer then?

The highest price you offer is 2/3 of the **HIRE** fee for that sized work.

You can of course buy for less.

## Now remember you will buy in bulk works that have not been sold.

For an artist you are a clearing house of unsold works.

You are doing them a service.

Their choice is some money or none.

## But they still have frames to use on new works.

Probably more importantly those frames have been paid for.

These frames are in a style of their choosing so this is a good arrangement.

## On the other hand you have unframed works.

They take far less storage space than framed works!

The works can be matted or remounted so they fit your standard frame sizes.

Then they blend with other work you hire in terms of size and frame style.

## The best source of stock for your art hiring program is elderly artists.

Keep in touch with these people and also seek out their friends.

Deceased estates of artists are another avenue for bulk purchases.

Keep track of those elderly artists and the deceased estate will eventuate.

## It doesn't matter what the retail price of a work is or was.

That might matter if you are selling the works.

But you are not doing that for they are hired and the payment is for their use.

## What is your hiring fee anyway?

All works hired are at a rate determined by their size.

Thus if you have five standard sizes then you have five standard fees.

Also **whatever you pay you are out of pocket until the work is hired.** So if you can obtain unwanted works **FREE** that is the best price.

## 8. Additional notes.

**This is additional to previous advice on hiring artwork.**
It is consistent with my advice on pricing artworks for sale.
Use anything you might find useful.

**If you hire your own artwork there are limits to expanding your income.**
Some potential hirers may not like what you do.
In addition it takes time to paint additional works.

**There may be better ways to spend that time.**
Expanding your hiring base for example.

**What if you buy other artists works?**
Then you can provide alternatives to your own work.
You can have many more works available to choose from than otherwise.

**But buying other artist's works can be expensive!**
Well it all depends what you buy and also how you do it.

**Most artists have many unsold works (but yours are for hiring).**
You can make an offer for these works by other artists.
At present they (those works) are otherwise not earning the artist any money.
In fact they have cost time and money already.

**The major money component of an unsold work is the frame.**
Any artist can use those frames for other works and save buying new frames.
Recycling frames is actually common so many unsold works are unframed.

**Unframed works should be cheaper than if they are framed.**
This suits a seller as they can use the frames on new works and save money.

**This suits you too because buying unframed works is less expensive.**
But buying in bulk should be even more inexpensive.

**Then you remove a psychological problem from the seller.**
They are no longer reminded of unsold works.
**AND** also have frames available for new ones.

**But what do you pay?**
Well you must be able to hire the works and make money.
Your hiring fees are set according to the size of the works.
So your purchase offer is based on the same principle.

**What do you offer then?**
The highest you offer is 2/3 of the **HIRE** fee for that sized work.
**BUT** you can buy for less.

**BUT remember you will buy in bulk works that have not been sold.**
For an artist you are a clearing house of unsold works.
You are doing them a service.
Their choice is some money or none – a pretty easy choice isn't it?

**AND they still have frames to use on new works.**
Probably even more importantly for them those frames have been paid for.
The frames are in a style of their choosing so this is a good arrangement.

**On the other hand you have unframed works.**
They take far less storage space than framed works!
The works are matted or remounted so they fit your standard frame sizes.
Then they blend with other work you hire in terms of size and frame style.

**But there is a potential problem (for you).**
Ideally **ALL** works should fit your standard sized frames.
**BUT** many will not!
So what do you do about that situation?

**Cut them down so they do fit.**
That seems drastic.
It is.

**BUT paying money.**
**THEN** buying a frame to fit is **MUCH** more drastic.

**Many works can be trimmed and not lose their original appeal.**
But make sure you do not cut off the artist's signature.
Works on paper are matted so they fit one of your standard frames.

**But stretchers are a problem?**
Take the work off the stretcher and glue it onto a suitably sized panel.

**What is your hiring fee anyway?**
All works hired are at a rate determined by their size.
Thus if you have five standard sizes then you have five standard fees.

**It doesn't matter what the retail price of a work is or was.**
That might matter if you are selling the works.
But you are not doing that.
They are being hired and the payment is for their use.

**A good source of stock for your art hiring program is elderly artists.**
Keep in touch with these people and also seek out their friends.

**Deceased estates of artists are the best avenue for bulk purchases.**
Keep track of those elderly artists and the deceased estate will eventuate.
The relatives often will be very happy to turn them into cash.

# Chapter Five: Selling the hiring.

| | | | | | |
|---|---|---|---|---|---|
| 1. | You | still | have | to | sell! |
| 2. | | Let's | | start | right! |
| 3. | How | do | you | sell | to | business? |
| 4. | What | is | your | main | objective? |
| 5. | | Testimonials | | help | too! |
| 6. | Do | you | have | an | action | plan? |
| 7. | Are you | making | best | use | of their | business cards? |
| 8. | How | successful | are | your | presentations? |
| 9. | | A | | | promotion: |

## 1. You still have to sell!

**Lots of people like being an artist but hate selling!**
The usual reason is thought to be a fear of rejection.
It's more likely that not everyone will buy every time someone asks them to.
There is personal effort that has to be invested in the selling process.
So this can make it seem personal to the seller.

**Another reason people are reluctant to sell is it is seen as an intrusion.**
The seller is taking up another person's time.
Is your career so unimportant it's not worth someone spend a little time?
They find out if they might like to buy a painting or use your hire service.
If that's the case then you are in the wrong business!

**You do someone a favour offering to sell or do something for them.**
Careful preparation and sensitive manner makes people appreciate your help.
They are very unlikely to reject it as an intrusion.
Permission marketing avoids any hint of coming on too strong, or rejection.
It also works very well.

**Sometimes selling doesn't seem important so we let other people do it.**
We deal with the important things like painting, and framing perhaps.

**A result of these so-called barriers to selling is people give up too soon.**
Research by Harvard University has salespeople give up after two attempts.
The same research said actual purchases are after five (or more) failures.
Harvard figures are averages so there is wide variation in the statistics.
Low priced purchases may indeed be bought at the first sales encounter.
But this is buying at a supermarket.

**On the other hand the more complex the sale.**
Also more expensive to the buyer, not just in money but also in status.
The more sales encounters there are likely to be.

**Do you suppose most people actually buy artwork first time they see it?**
It does happen but not very often.
When I ran a gallery people often came in a number of times before deciding.
What about hiring?

**Timing, persistence and patience are the keys to successful selling.**
This applies to hiring just as much as an outright sale of one of your works.
You need to sell the idea of hiring before you build this aspect of your career.

## 2 Let's start right?

**Having suitable selling strategies is the key to sales success.**
It's not good enough to make it up during the sales encounter.
Artists and quite a few gallery people tend to do this.

**Buying and selling is more complex than that.**
In particular, if you want to sell to business, you must have strategies.
Business decisions are often made by a number of people in an organization.
There's the boss's secretary, the boss's wife, and even the boss himself.
In big places purchasing officer, accounts department, CEO, board members.

**Possibly they don't talk to one another often, or in sometimes, not at all!**
How do you get to all these people to sell a work or hire anything?
It can be done, because businesses do buy artworks.
Some gallery people, and a few artists, specialize in this kind of market.
They experience excellent rewards for their efforts.

**One thing all have in common is a process that they follow.**
Standard (for them) ways of making their market aware of what they offer.
Follow up assumes there is a number of people to meet and get support from.
Only then will a final decision be made.
They do not expect to rock into a business with a portfolio and make a sale.
It just doesn't happen like that!

**Business-to-business marketing is just marketing to consumers.**
**EXCEPT** they have a corporation or company to pay for what they buy.
Marketing to government is much the same.

**Your best clients are worth far more than your average clients.**
Anticipated, personal, relevant marketing does better than unsolicited junk.
Making promises and keeping them is a great way to build your credibility.
You can't fool all the people, not even most of the time.

**Marketing that works is marketing that people choose to notice.**
People all over the world and at every income level, respond to marketing.
Provided it promises and delivers basic human wants.
Marketing is not an emergency measure.
Planned, thoughtful it started a long time ago and doesn't end until you finish.
Marketing begins before the painting commences.

**People don't buy what they need, they buy what they want!**
People want the extra, emotional bonus they get with what they love.
For artists, the share you get of someone's wallet is a measure of success.

**Good marketers tell a story.**
Effective stories link to the world view of the people who are listening.
Living and breathing an authentic story is the way to survive.
In a conversation rich world.
Reminding a prospect of a story they know and trust is a powerful shortcut.

### 3. How do you sell to business?

**What do you look at every day?**
Ask the prospect what is on the wall right in front of their desk.
That's what they look at every day they're at work.
A business-person spends a lot of time looking at that wall!
Surely it's worth spending some money on?
Artwork on an office wall make a difference to an impression visitors gain.

**Office decoration is not frivolity, but just good business sense!**
Is a prospect doing all they can to welcome potential clients and visitors?
What sort of impression does their business convey to the outside world?
What do people see as they enter the front door?
Does it give a right message to not just visitors but those who work there too?

**Could artworks improve productivity?**
Artworks on a wall make a positive visual statement.
They say we are not just concerned about business.
We foster some of the finer things in life too.
A well-chosen artwork creates a perfect atmosphere in a reception area.
In the main workplace, it keeps everyone happier and more peaceful
Happy workers are more productive than agitated, restless people.
Staring at bare walls is not likely to induce enthusiasm and good-feelings.

**Can art be therapeutic?**
This is an extension on the productivity theme.
Art hung in hospitals, creates an environment more pleasant and restful.
**This is not just for patients, but also staff and visitors.**
These people spend long periods in this environment, often stress-related.
It makes sense to reduce the tension as much as possible using passive aids
If a prospect works long hours in an office, it's worth being more appealing.

**Colour has a powerful effect on human psychology.**
Blue is believed to have a calming effect, whilst red triggers aggression.
Your work can be matched to the needs of the business-person this way.

**Suggest framing choices, or alternative artworks.**

The colour guide will be determined by the prospect.

**Won't it cost a fortune?**

It certainly could and that's why your prospect should have art on that wall.
Art gives an impression of success and status.
If this is important to a business, they need original artworks on the walls.
Fortunately the works do not have to be expensive, just look as if they are.
This may involve only quality framing.
It is possible for you to hire or rent out artworks for a fraction of the real price.

**Are you interested in making sales to business?**

Corporations buy all manner of artworks and some of it is for boardrooms.
Often this is quite large and prestigious (i.e. they pay a lot of money).

**Business buys smaller, less expensive works for corridors or offices.**

Cover the range of possibilities, including prints for the more public areas.
These days most businesses have little money to waste.
They are thus less inclined to splurge on artworks than a few years ago.

**Many people confuse leasing with hiring.**

The two are legal terms and have quite different taxation implications.
Leasing is like buying on hire purchase, but the deposit/residual is at the end.
Hiring is paying for use and no question of eventual purchase and ownership.
If the tax office thinks a client will buy, the taxation aspect isn't as attractive.

**So how does leasing work?**

A client leases paintings from a finance company, who bought it from you.
At the end of the lease term the finance company still owns the works.
They may sell them to their client for an additional payment (residual).
Find a finance company who will do this and you can offer this service.
They will pay more, but it is tax deductible if they're in business.
It will not matter whether they're prints or paintings; the process is the same.

**What's the catch?**

The only problem with this is that you'll not make much money.

You will need to lease out many works.

This is possible if you find hotels, motels and office blocks that need artwork.

There are some very large firms who do this already.

**A better option is hiring (renting).**

Here people pay so much, usually per month, for the use of the paintings.

It makes a great deal of sense to do this if it's at all possible.

**I prefer to hire, rather than sell my own works.**

I had a number of works hired for over 17 years by a firm of solicitors.

Depending how you calculate fees, actual costs are covered in a year or two.

Everything from then on is pure profit, and you still own the works!

If you have enough works hired out, you have a regular income stream.

This irons out the ebb and flow of normal art-world business transactions.

Old unsold works (everybody has some) can be part of your hire stock.

They are hired at the same hire price, as any similarly priced and sized work.
You'll need contracts to protect against damage, loss, non-payment etc.

## 4. What is your main objective?

**When you contact a prospect you don't just have a conversation.**
You begin negotiation intended to have them consider hiring artworks.
Before you start you obviously need to know what it is that you wish to do.

**It's surprising people enter negotiations without considering this.**
Can you imagine a trade union not knowing what they want if bargaining?

**You decide what you want, but you must know what they are.**
There may be a number of objectives that are important to you.
In this case write them down before you start.

**Once you have listed your objectives then prioritize them.**
At the top of your list will be the most important objective, and then so on.
Eventually you are really just dealing in wishes.
Priority: price, quality, comfort, style, economy, reliability, performance, size.
Someone else: style, performance, size, quality, price, and comfort.
Another: previous experience, quality, size, style, servicing, and economy.

**They are likely to buy different cars, but that's not really the point here.**
Importantly each knows what they want and how they might compromise.
They're prepared for actually looking at a car and talking to a salesman.
They're less likely to wonder next week, why they bought a particular car.

**Now the same situation faces you in your artistic life.**
Let's say you are talking with a prospective hirer about your works.
What is your main objective?
Do you want to get as much as possible for the hiring contract?
Perhaps you'd like to get works out of your hire storage and earn something?
Will this hiring sale help your long-term plans?
Do you have standard procedures to approach each hiring the same way?
Do you know what to do if they ask for a discount for example?

**Think of different typical negotiating situations.**

You can now write a list in priority order of your objectives for each one.

## 5. Testimonials help too!

**You should use testimonials whenever possible.**
They establish your credibility and win over potential clients.
They're more impressed by what people like them say than a CV.
Yes even more than any major award you have won!

**Never underestimate the power of a good testimonial!**
Post reviews and comments from satisfied clients on your website.
That increases credibility in the eyes of visitors.

**It encourages sales from first-time prospects if in printed material.**
An effective testimonial convinces readers you do exactly what you promise.
Especially if you are new to them and don't yet have a wide reputation.

**Here's how to gather quality testimonials:**
Have you already have some positive feedback from hiring clients?
Ask their permission to include their comments in your promotions.
Choose testimonials that tell prospects exactly what they can expect to gain.

**Every testimonial should have a first name, last name, and location.**
That information proves the recommendations are coming from real people.
I've only had one person who wasn't delighted to provide that permission.
I'm not writing for an academic audience so I didn't use her reference.

**If you have a website you may need to encourage new testimonials.**
Add a link to a form that allows clients to give you a vote of confidence.
'Click here to tell us what you think about the new artwork in your office!'

**Contact clients after they hire paintings to ask how they're received.**
Clients may send you glowing praise in a letter or email.
Then ask for permission to add it to your website or promotional material.
Do this although you do not then know exactly where to use a testimonial.
There's always somewhere that's appropriate.

**What if you don't have any testimonials yet?**
Offer free or reduced price hiring to some clients in exchange for thoughts.
They tell you about your hiring process and how it was received in their work.

**Once you've accumulated some good testimonials, use them.**
There should be testimonials included in any written material.

**Put your best testimonials on your website homepage.**
Other testimonials can be in the middle of your sales copy.

**Creating a page featuring only testimonials has limited effectiveness.**
People can skip this page or many of the testimonials.
Testimonials on each page of your website, is much more effective.
In addition they can be relevant to what is on that page.

**Do you collect testimonials?**
Get into the habit – it's a bit like collecting autographs - it's that simple!

## 6. Do you have an action plan?

An action plan is different from a plan.
A plan is a map which shows various elements of what you want to achieve.
An action plan has a sequence of steps that lets you put things together.
Then you do actually arrive at your destination or goal.

### Outline a starting point:
Take time to honestly evaluate your current situation.
Also consider your skills, and then decide which areas need improving.
Consider just how you will improve those areas.

### Write down your goals in a priority order.
The most important and urgent are placed first.
Then the most important, followed by urgent and everything else after that.

### Develop your plan by working out just what you want to do.
This will help you take control of your present situation.
You can then shape up your future in the way you want it to go.

### Decide how you'll deal with setbacks:
Dealing with reverses is never easy, but they are inevitable.
If you are prepared, then they become manageable at least.

### Set milestones by breaking down the overall plan into smaller sections.
Set target dates for when each of the sections will be reached and passed.

### Develop a reward system:
As each smaller goal is reached, reward yourself and continue on your path.

### At regular intervals, review what you have achieved.
Make important changes to adjust your plan according to a new perspective.

## 7. Are you making best use of their business card?

**Just about every business and business person has a business card.**
You should get into the habit of collecting these little pieces of cardboard.
Card people are potential hirers for their business or know someone who is.

**These are people that you should cultivate so here's what you can do.**

**Take a walk down a nearby business precinct.**
As you pass step inside any that seem as if they need artworks on walls.
This could be walls you can't actually see (offices, boardrooms, hallways).

**There will usually be a reception desk in a prominent place.**
Behind the desk is a lady who answers the telephone and greets visitors.
There are also business cards arranged neatly on the counter in front of her.
They will belong to the partners of the business, key sales people and so on.

**Take one of each card.**
The receptionist will ask you what you are doing.
Tell her that you may need to contact someone about their wall decorations.
You are not selling art or art hiring at this point.

**Who would be the best person to contact about that?**
Note this on their business card.
Also make a note of the name of the receptionist.
Hopefully you will get to know her quite well.

**You will then leave after carefully looking around.**

**On your next contact with any place you visited mention:**
You called on (whenever) and talked to (receptionist) about wall decorations.
Ask if you could contact (whoever) to discuss ideas they may not have had.

**This contact could be by phone, or email.**

All you seek at this point is permission to make more contacts.

You'd like an appointment for a short meeting with someone.

It will be about their wall decorations.

You do not mention what you have in mind over the phone.
Do that and you will not get an appointment!

## 8. How successful are your presentations?

**You are about to meet a prospective hiring client.**
You'll be showing one or more of works and hoping to finalize arrangements.
What will you do?

**People buy most things emotionally THEN rationalize their purchase.**
That lets them explain the purchase to others (or themselves).
Intuition comes before thinking but only for buyers (or hirers)!

**Sellers (you) should know exactly what you are doing.**
Plan as carefully as for any other important business presentation.
Because that's what it is.

**Let's assume you are appealing to the right person (or time is wasted).**
You are making a presentation to one or more key decision-makers.
So start in a small way.
There's no need to be smart, trendy or let them know what you know.
It's a good idea to play dumb.
Use the Columbo (TV detective) strategy – 'By the way …?
The prospect will reveal all you need to know about how they feel.

**Listen for 'but' – whatever comes next is important.**
Observation is more reliable than listening like Columbo see what happens.
Then analyse what you see and hear for clues to the overall picture.

**Set the stage.**
Make the prospect know you are confident – a winner.
The perception is the reality.

**Rehearse so the presentation flows effortlessly.**
Go low-tech – don't assume any equipment will work.
Check all details and modify as needed to improve your presentation.
Avoid complacency.

**Know your audience and assume nothing**
Research your client's business and personal background.
In your presentation relate to the people who are there.

**Have a warm-up act.**
Establish an emotional link before rational discussion etc.
Create trust by getting 'on-side' which could be suitable humour.

**Pull out all stops!**
This must be an entertaining presentation.
You must look interested.

**Watch for the glazed eyes.**
If the presentation is not working then go to Plan B
So have Plan B practiced and ready to roll.

**Save best for last.**
Bring out the **BIG** idea.
Don't have any handouts they must experience the **BIG** idea.
Take them through the journey you went through getting the **BIG** idea.

**Have an encore ready.**
Another way of reaching the client.

**Did you engage, entertain and enlighten?**
Do you have several presentations ready to roll?
Write out a script or two and practice them.

## 9. A promotion:

**The purpose of hiring art is so your place is attractive for business.**
Research says 70-80% of client impression of a business is on what is seen.
Artworks help create a pleasant work environment.
This adds to the happiness, and thus productivity, of your employees.
Do employees do small things to make a workplace personal and pleasant?
That's part of the same psychology!

**Show clients they have taste and judgment and deserve the best.**
That's when you hang artworks in areas that are client focused,
Even if clients don't like an individual work they appreciate original paintings.

**Your reception area can have paintings related to your line of business.**
Like beef and vegetables in a MacDonald's restaurant.
Change the look of a business without major renovation costs or upheavals.
Hang paintings in strategic spots you alter the appearance of your business.
And we'll do the hanging for you too!

**Small monthly payments are a fraction of what you would if bought.**
The exact cost depends on the works you select.
Rental varies according to the artist and the size of the work.

**If you tire of the artworks you have selected then redecorate...**
Change the artworks ... in many cases at little or no additional cost.
The small monthly payment mean you pay less than for a renovation.

**You can legally claim your hiring costs as a full tax deduction.**
But your place of business will have a prestige image.
That's because original and quality artworks are part of the environment.

**So you can see ... hiring paintings makes good business sense!**
Contact my studio or gallery to ask about our introductory hire offer.
This offer is only available to Chamber of Commerce (or other organization).
If you are a member then contact me during May (or whenever).

**Check out renting or buying for businesses with a tax accountant.** Then you'll be knowledgeable and prepared when it is discussed.

# Chapter Six: Tools.

1. A possible initial letter to a hiring prospect.
2. An example of a follow-up phone call.
3. Documentation is important.
4. Do you keep photographic records?
5. Contracts are essential.
6. Suggested CONTRACT duration and related charges:
7. Sample monthly invoice to hirer.

## 1. A possible initial letter to a hiring prospect.

**A sample letter that could be sent to a prospect for your hiring services.**
Change this to suit your way of doing things.

### Are any of these problems yours?
You'd like to freshen your business image but don't know how.
You'd like to attract more clients to your business.
You'd like art in your business but can't afford it.

### If so.....
Please complete the following and return to: Joe Bloggs (you),
4 Palette Street (your address), (rest of address)
Don't forget your phone number, fax and email address!

......................................................................................

**YOUR DETAILS:**

| | |
|---|---|
| Name(s): | Title(s): Business: |
| Address: | Town/City/Suburb: |
| State: | Postcode: |
| Work phone: | Best time to ring: |
| Home phone: | Best time to ring: |
| Fax number: | Best time to send: |
| Email address: | |

**I am interested in finding out more about art hiring**
Signed:........................

## 2. An example of a follow-up phone call.

Good morning.....................
This is (you) from (wherever).

**I wrote to you last week about hiring original artwork for your business.
Is now a good time to talk about the letter?**

* **IF NO**:  I understand........
When would be a better time? ...................
So if I give you a call at ....... on.......... we can talk about it further.
Good. I'll do that.

* **IF YES:** How do you feel about the idea?
...............................................

Well, what did you think?
...............................................

**If positive:**
Would you like to see a sample of what we have available for hire? ..........

What if I brought a few of the paintings we have and you'll be able to decide
the sorts of paintings you like?
When would be a good time to do this? ....................
And then I can bring some paintings around for you to look at.
How does that all sound?
So I'll see you at ......... on..........................

**You could also email photographs.**
But that avoids any personal contact with the prospect.
Personal contact is preferable.
Use emailed images when actual works are being chosen for the business.

**If negative:**
That's fine.
Thank you for considering the plan.
I understand.
Thank you for sharing your thoughts with me.

By the way ... even though it isn't the thing for you,
Maybe you know of other people who might benefit from it.

We'd really be grateful if you shared the information with them.
Is there anyone who you think might be particularly interested?
.............................................

Well, thank you .......................................it's been nice talking to you.

## * IF THEY HAVEN'T HAD TIME TO READ LETTER, etc.

I understand..... you must get so much mail
**OR**
You've probably been very busy
Maybe I could just.... refresh your memory....

Highlight the main points
I guess the most important thing for you is you can have original artworks.
Hanging on your walls at a fraction of the cost of buying the works and....
You can claim the monthly payments as a tax deduction.
An important factor is they hang on the walls of your business.

**They look like your own possessions.**
Which means your clients admire them as part of your establishment.
And your employees get to enjoy them as well.

**OR**

When would be a good time to show you some of what is available for hire?
If necessary, suggest outside work hours ... early morning or after work?

This guide is an indication of the things that could be said over the phone.
Following an earlier communication by mail or fax or email.

The main thing is **NOT** to actually try and sell the hiring.
Gain an appointment so a prospect can view works in their business setting.
They are works that might be hired.

## 3. Documentation is important.

**Let's say you're just commencing your art hiring (renting) business.**
You need a system for keeping all the usual financial records.

**You also need a stock control program.**
As well as a client tracking system.

**Stock, means artworks and craft items that you have for hire.**
It is possible your accounting system will have a stock control component.
If so make use of it after reading these notes.
Usually accounting programs assume direct purchase of stock.

**Are you going to give each work a code number?**
If you have a bar-code system, the answer to this question is obvious.
Without this technology, there's still an argument for a code for each work.
The code can be printed and fixed to the rear of the work as a reference.
That helps you determine which work matches which set of records.

**The code could be artist's initials, or better first four letters of the name.**
There could be numbers representing the order each work was received.
This could be to three numerals so a first is 001, then 002 to 231, 232, etc.
You only need to adjust the database with 1,000th work from one artist.

**Any other system that makes sense to you will be just as good.**
But whatever you start with, stick to for it's not easy to change things later.

**Naturally you'll need to record the name of the artist.**
Both first and surname should be entered.
The title of the work is another piece of information that's essential.

**What medium was used?**
Use a shorthand for different media but keep the number of letters the same.
Perhaps 'etch' for etching, 'wcol' for water colour, 'past' for pastel, and so on.

**Size is also important.**
Record both framed and unframed sizes.
Use either metric or imperial measurements, but don't mix the two.
Is the work framed, for not all will be?

**Where is the work?**
It could be in your studio, on hire to a client, or stored somewhere else.
All this information needs a place to go.

A **work will never be for hire, sale, sold, or paid off at the same time.**
Its status is one or other of those situations.

**When did you receive or buy the work?**
From whom was it bought, if you purchase your stock?

**When was the work returned to the owner?**
That's if you are operating on consignment and did not hire the work?

**Closely related to this, who owns the work?**
It may be the artist, but it could be yourself or someone else (client or dealer).

**Say a hiring has been negotiated.**
Then you'll need to record the name of the hirer and the hire date.
Your receipt number will also be a handy reference to have.
Record the date of your payment to the owner.
Either before or after the hiring depending on whether you consign or not.
Also enter the cheque number of the payment.

**This system accommodates people making regular hire payments.**
You can show how much a client has paid and the due date for next payment.
Also record how much the artist (owner) has been paid and is still to receive.

**Finally what is the price of the work?**
This is the price your hiring calculations are based on.

**You'll need to enter the cost price too.**
Where discounts are offered they'll need to be in your system.

**Exactly how you set this up varies according to computer software.**
Do you have enough space to write a reasonable title and artist's name?
But dates only need eight spaces (--/--/--).

**Once you have your system in place do a test.**
Enter 10 artworks and print out the results.
You'll be surprised at how easy it is to make a mistake.
If it doesn't work properly, fix the system then do another test run.
If all goes to plan, then go ahead and enter whatever stock you have for hire.

**Print sheets, or cards with blanks that match your stock control system.**
When a new work arrives enter the details at that time.
You can provide a copy for the artist too.
Later the information can be transferred to your computer.

**If you can link this to your accounting and client systems, do so.**
It should be possible with modern software and some computer knowledge.
You may like to add other features too.
That's O.K. but there's no need to record information that'll never be used.

## 4. Do you keep photographic records?

**It makes sense to keep photographic records of your hiring stock.**
If digital it's easier to keep track of where the works are at a particular time.

### How are the photographs taken?
Here we will only be concerned with images of your hiring inventory.
Use slides, prints or digital images.
But eventually you'll have hundreds of photographs or images.
Your choice of medium limits in some way what you can do, so think ahead.

### Slides can be projected to life size.
Then the viewer obtains a very good idea of the painting's impact.
Also slides are best if you might want to make prints from a painting later.

### On the other hand coloured prints can be viewed by several people.
There is no need for a projector, or holding them up to a light source.

### Digital images are quick and easily sent to someone.
These days they can be printed in full colour too.
The photographs only need to be reasonable.
This isn't necessarily a standard you might need to make reproduction prints.

### Photographing framed work is hard, particularly pastel or watercolour.
Reflections are captured superbly in the glass.
But they are at the expense of the artistic image.
The darker the work, the more reflections create problems.
This is really a task for a professional photographer.

### Avoid the problem completely, take photographs before they're framed.
In future the very next thing you do after signing each completed painting.
Is to take a photograph.

**Thus you'll record all your completed works, but in an unframed state.**
You won't waste film on shots of frames this way either.
You could use a mat to provide a framed effect.

**Digital images can be stored as computer files, called up in any order.**
The images can be linked with written information about the painting.
This can be changed from time to time if needed (such as monthly fee).
Printing this material provides you with something for any potential client.
You can provide them with a copy too!

**File images by their hiring fee, subject matter, medium and size.**
You also need to record whether a work is currently on hire or is available.
You may like other criteria, these are likely to be concerns to a potential hirer.
Thus the same work can appear in different categories.

**Why do you need such a record?**
Photographs can substitute for paintings.
Shuffle images, rather than paintings, if selecting for a particular location.
This process reduces handling of actual works (some at the framers).
But you can still come up with the best combination for a prospective client.
It may be the only way to do this if works are stored in a variety of places.

**Write a message to accompany them.**
"Some possible works for your office along the lines of yesterday's discussion.
Let me know what you like and I'll bring them to your office for consideration".
They appreciate this, hiring sales come as clients, ask about particular works.
There's a bit of organization, but the cost is not as much as you'd expect.
Most importantly the reduced handling means less damage to your frames.

**Send the minimum number of works a client needs fora particular site.**
Once choices are made bring the real thing with a chance of a satisfied client.

**It is a major mistake to show too many works.**
This only promotes confusion and indecision.
They should see nothing that you do not want the person to see.

**Be selective.**
Have different presentations to each prospective client or outlet.
Usually work from hire stock of the kind and monthly fee to appeal to a hirer.

**If emailing photos limit the size of the entire email to under a megabyte.**
Recommended to keep download time minimal for broadband connections.
Also to keep download time reasonable for those with dial up.

**After taking digital photographs, it's a good idea to edit on a computer.**
Crop extraneous information and do after-the-fact colour correction.
You can use photo editing software Adobe Photo Deluxe, Adobe Photoshop.
I'm not covering all features of the program but a few are worth discussing:

**The first operation on your photo that you should do is to crop.**
Cropping is to remove the space around your art in the photograph.
The tighter the crop when you originally took the photograph the better.
But removing extraneous information in post-processing is a must.

**A marquee tool crops the part of the photograph you wish to keep.**
Then select the crop command from a menu.
Digital camera programs have a crop tool to draw box around what you want.
Make your crop tight but be sure not to crop out any of your artwork.

**The way to correct colours varies dramatically between programs.**
Using a photo editing program's auto colour correction is your best bet.
This command determines the extents of the colours captured in your photo.
It tweaks boundaries to make sure the white and black point is correctly set.
The process isn't without its flaws, but often the result is good.
You are the expert on your art, so if the colour looks wrong, undo it.

**A final operation before you email a digital photo is resize it suitably.**
Show a work on a computer screen and not print larger than 3' x 5' for hiring.
A resolution of 800x800@ 150dpi accurately displays a work and file size low.

**Reduce the dimensions, but there is a risk of losing a quality image.**
To print a photograph, it is best to leave the image at its original resolution.

**Resize a photograph, get the image size command.**
It's in the photo editing software.
This command is often under the image menu if your program has one.
If you've option to set the resolution and DPI, use the numbers listed before.
Depending on enter for either the width or height the size you want it to be.
Only enter one dimension, the other changes based on the original ratio.
Make sure that 'constrain proportions' is enabled (if the option is given).
You only wish to scale a photograph, not distort the height/ width ratio.

**Once you've made all the changes to your photograph, save your file.**
It's good practice to save the edited file as something different from original.
Keep the original intact especially if sizing down or making substantial edits.

**You may have the option of which file-type you wish to save as.**
Jpeg provides good quality with a small size; what you want if emailing.
If you're unconcerned with file size and want best quality, use TIFF files.

**Now you're ready to email your photo(s).**
Open a new message with your email program, and attach the hiring files.
The attach files command varies between programs.
Once you find and click, it goes to a dialog box so you to select which files.
Find the files you edited, and click OK.
Compose a message for this email, and send away to your hiring prospect.

## 5. Contracts are essential.

### Contracts spell out the behaviour expected of both parties.
They make misunderstandings less likely (if all is covered and understood).
A documented contract can be shown to others for comments and advice.
Word of mouth changes as circumstances change or memory is less reliable.
This can apply to you just as much as anyone else.

### Develop your own contract.
Put in the things you expect from a client, as well as the things you'll do.
Outline who does what and any special requirements you might have.

### It's better to identify problems early, for often they can be resolved.
Provision of a contract allows you to do that.
Negotiate, if they won't sign on terms you consider a basic minimum, leave.
Keep in mind most business owners are honest struggling people.
It's no easier being a business owner than an artist; just more expensive!

### A sample contract based on one I used when hiring art from my gallery.

*Art Professional Marketing*
*14 Kennedy Avenue WAGGA WAGGA NSW 2650*
*ABN (whatever)*

### HIRE OF ARTWORK CONTRACT
*This contract is made in duplicate on the (date) twelfth day of August, 2016 at (city) Wagga Wagga in the State of New South Wales, BETWEEN (your company) Hiring Gallery P/L (hereinafter called the OWNER) whose agent is (your business) Art Professional Marketing, 14 Kennedy Avenue, Wagga Wagga AND (insert name of the hiring business here) (hereinafter called the HIRER).*

**DESCRIPTION OF WORK(S):**
This could be simple (like below) or more detailed, you decide.
'At Dinner' by Graeme Smith
'Kinchiga Interior' by Clark Barrett
'Abandoned Farm' by James Wynne

**USE:**
The works described above may be used in any way desired by the Hirer except that they may not be damaged nor resold.

**FEE:**
Shall be $49.50 per month, commencing on the first day of September, 2021, and payable in equal monthly payments in advance by the Hirer on the first day of every month to the Owner/Agent at his above address, or any other reasonable place as he notifies in writing.

**TERM:**
The duration of the contract shall be 12 months, commencing on the first day of September, 2020 and terminating on the 31st day of August, 2021.

**OPTIONS:**
The hirer may pay annually instead of monthly. In that case the annual fee of $445.50 shall be payable on 1st September 2020.

The hirer may allow the owner to choose which works are to be hired. In that case the annual or monthly fee is reduced by 10%.

Subject to satisfactory completion of this contract the Owner/Agent and the Hirer may agree to continue the contract on a monthly or annual basis.

## CONDITIONS:

The Hirer agrees to compensate and meet all claims of the Owner for the loss or damage to part or whole of the artworks as a result of any accident, or neglect, or a deliberate or careless act, or a breach of any condition of the contract by the Hirer, his employee or agents, or any person handling the artworks with the consent of the Hirer, his employees or agent.

Where the Hirer unlawfully remains in possession of the artworks after termination of the contract, the Owner/Agent is entitled, in addition to any other claim, to payments equal to the monthly fee as compensation for use and possession of the artworks.

There shall be no increase in charges from those specified above, except where additional work(s) are hired during the term of this contract. Notice of such additional works, the new charges and the commencing date shall be attached to this contract.

    a) Upon termination or completion of the contract for any cause, the Hirer shall promptly and peacefully give possession of the artworks in the condition and state of repair required by this contract.

    b) The Owner/Agent shall have right to enter premises peacefully to regain possession of the artworks or to continue the contract on a month to month or annual basis:

        i) Where the Hirer has failed to pay the monthly fee for a period in excess of twenty- eight (28) days, whether formally demanded or not.

        ii) Where the Hirer has seriously or persistently breached any condition of this contract.

        iii) Upon the Hirer being declared bankrupt or insolvent according to law, or making any assignment for the benefit of creditors.

IN WITNESS whereof the parties hereto have hereunto executed these presents the day and year first hereinbefore written. (I copied this from a real estate rental contract).

*SIGNED by the OWNER or his Agent}*

     *in the presence of:*
     *SIGNED by the HIRER}*
     *in the presence of:*
     *DATE:*

## 6. Suggested CONTRACT duration and related charges:

**LESS THAN 36 MONTHS:**
Maximum of 2% per month of current value of work at time of hiring.

**MORE THAN 36 MONTHS:**
Maximum of 1.5% per month of current value of work at time of hiring.

**The real cost of hiring is not as great as often thought.**
The outlay is reduced by the business tax rate (which varies).
Tax is claimed at the full hiring amount as it's a legitimate business expense.
Not as a reduced `buy-out' figure (as in leasing).
Interest on money not spent (varies), appreciation of artworks, inflation rate.

**An actual example:**
Original cost = $450 per painting for 4 paintings (not mine that's what I paid).
Hire = ($9 per painting per month) $36 per month payment for 18 months.
But $3.15 per painting per month was tax deductible at a rate of 35%
Real hiring cost = ($9 - $3.15 = $5.85 a painting a month) or $23.40 a month.

**There is no extra for rises in value of paintings during hiring period.**
So several years down the track the client could be hiring four $900 works.
But the actual outlay is still $23.40 per month (calculated value was $450 ea..

**Later reduce long-term client's fees further as illustrated previously.**
But it may only be necessary to point out the capital gains values (as above).
That demonstrates the increasing value to the client of continued hiring.
It will cost more to replace these works with equivalent valued works!

## 7. Sample monthly invoice to hirer.

*Art Professional Marketing*
*14 Kennedy Avenue WAGGA WAGGA NSW 2650*
ABN (whatever)
**Joe Bloggs**
**Joe Bloggs & Associates**
**PO Box xx**
**WAGGA WAGGA, NSW 2650**

**Tax Invoice 11/12/2019**
**DESCRIPTION AMOUNT**

---

| | |
|---|---|
| Art hiring for 12 months @ $445.50 per annum. | $445.50 |
| Less 10% hirer's choice of works | $ 44.55 |

---

**TOTAL: $400.95**

| | |
|---|---|
| Paid from the previous invoice …. | $178.20 |
| Thank you. | |

**Payments after 11/12/2019 are not included in this statement.**
**Please make payment to (your company).**

**10% GST ($36.45) is included in your annual hire fee**

Best wishes,

(Graeme Smith)

**Payments may be made direct into our account:**
Your company
Your account number
Your bank details.

# Chapter Seven: Wrapping up.

### 1. Just how will your works be best marketed?
### 2. Could you use Ken Done's approach?


## 1. Just how will your works be best marketed?

**Not only do you complete the works there's all that marketing stuff too!**
You **MUST** make time for the marketing and selling as they're your business.
Then things can change because your mind-set will be different.
You will probably resist this at first due to accumulated experience and habit.
Like most other artists you are used to doing things in a certain way.
This way is just the same as all the other artists!
You think about yourself as an artist rather than as a business person.

**Some years ago I painted works for a horse racing themed exhibition.**
Horses, jockeys, bookies, people in crowds and all the things you'd expect.
I was pleased with what I had done and anticipated a good sales result.
Particularly as I had involved racing people with the exhibition.
The exhibition looked great, lots of people loved the paintings but **none** sold.

**I tried again on Melbourne Cup day.**
This exhibition was at the racecourse where a meeting was being held.
The result was a little better for I sold one work.
A small watercolour to the bookie who was the subject of the painting.

**But I did receive two commissions for paintings of race horses.**
I got thinking about commissions and painting horses.

**There are certain kinds of paintings that are mainly commissioned.**
Having exhibitions of this kind of work will usually fail.

**They won' fail due to inferior work but by being not specific enough.**
The more specific the work the fewer buyers there are.

**But more appealing to a particular buyer.**
AND
They commission such works.
They also pay higher prices!

**Commissioned works can also be hired.**
When that happens they tend to be hired for a **VERY** long time.
It is well-worth painting commissions for this purpose.

## 2. Could you use Ken Done's approach?

**Australian readers will be familiar with Ken Done.**
I encountered an article on Ken in a business magazine.
I have summarized it.
For Ken the business is as serious as the painting.
He knows how hard it is to run a business and unforgiving the marketplace.
His first exhibition was at 40 and has built a multi-million dollar business.
At the time of this article Ken had 10 shops and licensing arrangements.
They are with major clothing and design companies throughout the world.
They sell his art and related products.
He had 50 one-man exhibitions internationally in Australia, Japan & France.

**He opened his first gallery in 1980 (just after the first exhibition).**
He made 12 blue on white T-Shirts to give to the press.
They were simple drawings he'd done of Sydney Harbour.
The response was such that people rang asking about them next day.
People from Vogue magazine wanted more and others wrote about them.

**One was hung on a coat hanger in a tree outside the new gallery.**
There was a hand written sign "Sydney Harbour T-shirt $10".
Some were in a basket in a hallway and Ken waited to see if they sold.
Well in the next twenty years, people have bought around $8 million worth!

**For Ken it's all about making a drawing good enough for an art gallery.**
Then repeating that effort by putting it on something wearable.
Having consumers interested enough to buy that and walk around with it on!

**The success of his business is actually more complex than that.**
It has a lot to do with a surge in national pride during the early eighties.
At that time there probably wasn't anything else to buy, which said Sydney.
Done thinks it has a great deal to do with his creativity as well.

**After this beginning he opened a shop in the centre of Sydney.**
He sold T-shirts and other similar items ad later, further outlets also opened.
Then people approached Done for licences for his designs on their products.
These were also set up with manufacturing companies in America and Japan.

**Now Ken controls the operation without licensed assistance.**
He wanted more time to paint and not interested in growth for its own sake.
When this article was written (2000) he was developing a range of products.
These included home wares, plates, cups, beach towels and similar items.
100,000 of each design is produced and sold!
His business also exports, with Hawaii and Japan being two major markets.

**How does he do it all you might ask?**
90% of Ken Done's time is spent painting.
That's on any day except Monday when he plays golf.
He expects to do some of his best work in the next few years.

**People separate Ken Done from what Ken Done's business does.**
His wife and children all work in the business.
The family business concerns itself with making the very best product it can.
They make it in Australia whenever possible.
They also deal with the concept of selling intellectual property.

**Done says: "I've always seen business as the most creative thing".**
"You're putting together lots of disparate people to make something happen.
I didn't ever plan for success; I just got on with it."
So should you!

# WHERE NEXT:

BUT being a professional artist is NOW harder than it ever was.
These books are on earning money from a professional art career.

Gallery Co-Operation
http://www.amazon.com/dp/B087637FFW

**Selling Strategies**
http://www.amazon.com/dp/B0882JH3WN

**Copyright**
http://www.amazon.com/dp/B0892HWYTV

Make Exhibitions Work
http://www.amazon.com/dp/B0882MFPGX

Agents
http://www.amazon.com/dp/B08847Y9KS

**Your Website**
http://www.amazon.com/dp/B08846SWQP

Courses and Workshops
http://www.amazon.com/dp/B0884B51JB

Selling Prints
http://www.amazon.com/dp/B08846SWQW

Retirement
http://www.amazon.com/dp/B0884D9TBP

Art School
http://www.amazon.com/dp/B08849FV59


BUT being a professional artist is NOW harder than it ever was.
This book is the last of a series on earning real money.
From a professional art career.

**TAKE THE PLUNGE and Consider a Gallery.**
http://www.amazon.com/dp/B0874JF964
Hardback
http://www.amazon.com/dp/B09GQRB34T

# NOT NOW:

Perhaps one of these books could interest you then?

**What about your own memories?**
**YOU** could publish them – like I did!
http://www.amazon.com/dp/B087DWKPTP

**A simple way to start developing creativity.**
If you are a parent, teacher or someone who meets a group regularly?
http://www.amazon.com/dp/B088T1KFQZ

**The way most people start to become an artist!**
http://www.amazon.com/dp/B088Y1DPL6

**About some more of my memories.**
http://www.amazon.com/dp/B088Y4RPL9

# SEND TO:

**Know anyone interested in** chocolate recipes?
**Send them a link then.**

http://www.amazon.com/dp/B0882HK9Q9


**Know anyone interested in THIS book?**
**HIRING beats selling!**
http://www.amazon.com/dp/B0884JWR2S

www.ingramcontent.com/pod-product-compliance
Lightning Source LLC
Chambersburg PA
CBHW020552220526
45463CB00006B/2273